CULTURE ENCYCLOPEDIA

ART

CULTURE ENCYCLOPEDIA

ART

Antony Mason

Mason Crest

Mason Crest Publishers Inc.
370 Reed Road
Broomall, PA 19008
(866) MCP-BOOK (toll free)
www.masoncrest.com
This edition first published in 2003

First published by Miles Kelly Publishing,
Bardfield Centre, Great Bardfield, Essex, CM7 4SL, U.K.
Copyright © Miles Kelly Publishing 2002, 2003

2 4 6 8 10 9 7 5 3 1

Library of Congress Cataloging-in-Publication Data on file
at the Library of Congress

ISBN 1-59084-475-0

Author
Antony Mason

Designed and Edited by
Starry Dog Books

Project Editor
Belinda Gallagher

Assistant Editors
Mark Darling, Nicola Jessop, Isla Macuish

Artwork Commissioning
Lesley Cartlidge

Indexer
Jane Parker

Picture Research
Ruth Boardman, Liberty Newton

Color Reproduction
DPI Colour, Saffron Walden, Essex, UK

Printed in China

Contents

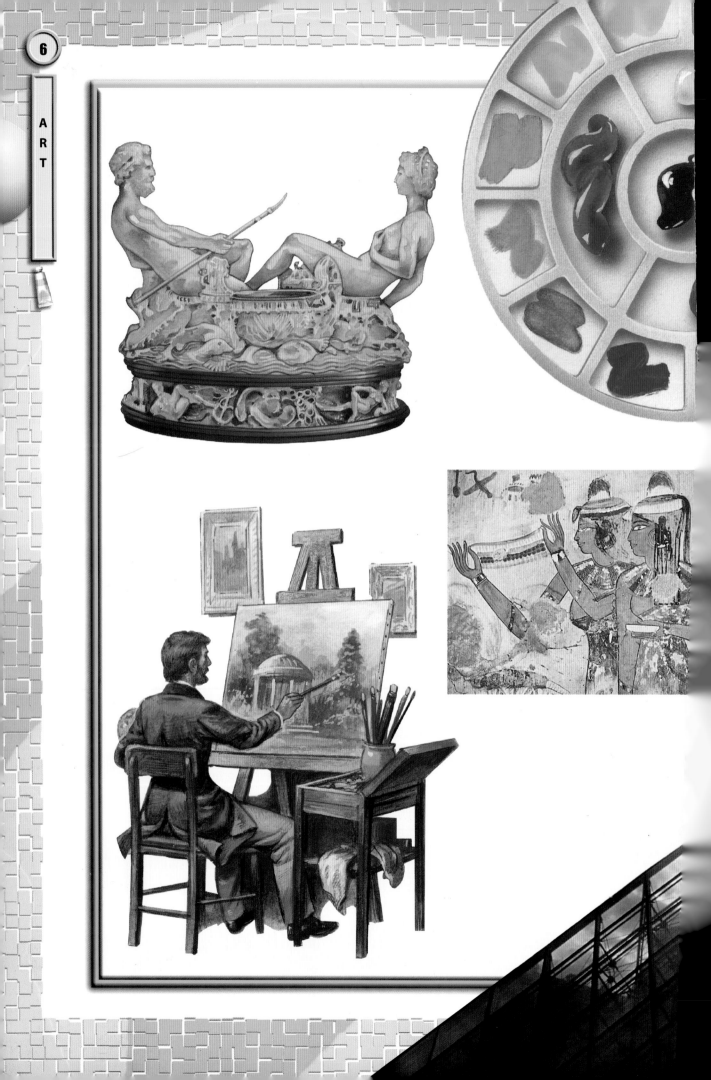

Art

EVERYONE has a favorite piece of art. It could be a painting you have at home, or a print of a famous painting by one of the great artists of the past. Or it could be a photograph in a book, or a sculpture in a park. There is something about that work of art that appeals to you in a special way, and makes you remember it. Art is about creating visual images, reordering dollops of paint, or a block of stone to produce something memorable. But art is more than simply something to look at and admire. It represents the personal vision of the artist, and offers a channel of communication between the artist and the viewer. Over the centuries, ideas about how this should be done have changed, providing us with an extraordinary historical record of the changing ways people have viewed the world.

Painting as decoration

MANY thousands of years before the very first civilizations developed in Mesopotamia, Egypt, and China, artists had begun to decorate the world in which they lived. We know this because paintings have been found on the walls of caves dating back to at least 18,000 BC. Painting is clearly a natural instinct of human beings. There are many reasons why artists paint, but one is to make our surroundings look more interesting, more personal and more beautiful.

◪ ROMAN MURAL
The Romans liked to decorate the insides of their houses with wall paintings, or "murals." Many murals were found in excellent condition in Pompeii—a Roman city near Naples that was buried under tons of ash when the volcano Vesuvius erupted in AD 79.

◪ ETHIOPIAN WALL PAINTING
Ethiopia was the first country in Africa to adopt Christianity, in AD 321, and ever since artists have painted the interior walls of churches with murals. The brightly colored pictures show figures from the Bible and later, Christian saints.

◪ THE LASCAUX CAVE PAINTINGS
In 1940, four French boys were searching for treasure in a cave near the Dordogne River in southwest France when they discovered some amazing prehistoric cave paintings. Made over 15,000 years ago, the paintings depict animals such as bison, deer, and horses.

▷ MINOAN MURALS

The Minoan civilization developed on Crete and neighboring Mediterranean islands from about 2200 BC, but collapsed after about 1100 BC. In recent years, archaeologists have unearthed a number of Minoan palaces, such as Knossos on Crete, and have found the remains of many colorful and lively murals that adorned their walls. This one is of a tree blowing in the wind.

◪ TRICKING THE EYE—TROMPE L'OEIL

By imitating stone and marble surfaces, and using clever shading techniques, artists discovered that they could transform a plain, flat wall into a convincing architectural feature, that appeared to have depth. Here, the Italian artist Paolo Veronese (1528–88) has created a country scene, viewed through an elaborate painted stone arch.

◪ MEXICAN MURALS

Wall paintings and mosaics (made of thousands of tiny glass-coated tiles) are sometimes used to decorate the outsides of buildings. The tradition is particularly strong in Mexico, as seen here at Mexico City University. Most old murals are found on inside walls, mainly because murals on outside walls are gradually destroyed by the weather.

POTTERY

It is not just walls that are decorated with paintings. Since ancient times, pottery has been beautifully painted with patterns and pictures, ranging from simple geometric designs to elaborate and complex scenes, including figures and landscapes.

Religious art

THE history of art is closely linked to religion. Painting was used to decorate places of worship, such as Buddhist and Hindu temples, and Christian churches. This was partly to make them the most attractive places in the community, as a way of showing respect and reverence for the gods. But it was also a way of teaching worshipers about stories from the scriptures—especially useful in the days when not many people could read. Religious communities were often wealthy, and could pay for the best artists of the day to work for them.

◩ ILLUMINATED MANUSCRIPT

In medieval Europe, most books were produced by Christian monks. They wrote the books out by hand, and illustrated them with colorful paintings, called "illuminations." Many of the early skills of European painting were learned through manuscript illumination.

◩ EGYPTIAN TOMB PAINTING

The ancient Egyptians decorated the inside walls of their tombs with elaborate paintings depicting the lives of the dead. This was a way of affirming their belief that the dead person would continue to lead a similar life in the afterworld. Faces are always shown with the head turned sideways, "in profile."

▱ TIBETAN TANKA

Buddhist temple hangings from Tibet are known as "tankas." Painted onto canvas following strict rules, they show gods, holy beings, and sacred symbols. The images are considered sacred, and are designed to help worshipers pray. Here, the 11th-century saint Milarepa is seen surrounded by his disciples.

⚀ ICONS

Icons are sacred images, usually painted on wood, made for the Christian Orthodox Church. They show figures from the Christian scriptures and saints. The two saints in this 16th-century icon founded a monastery in Russia. Icons are believed to provide a precious channel of communication between worshipers and God.

⚀ GIOTTO

One of the great early European painters was the Italian Giotto di Bodone (c.1267–1337). He decorated the walls of the Scrovegni Chapel in Padua with a series of scenes from the life of Christ. In *The Raising of Lazarus*, Christ is seen bringing the dead Lazarus back to life.

MUSLIM PATTERNS

In Islam, it is forbidden to paint pictures of people or animals. So artists decorate the mosques and holy books with beautiful and intricate geometric patterns.

⚀ STAINED GLASS

In medieval times, Christian churches were the grandest buildings in Europe, filled with paintings and treasures. Colored, or "stained," glass windows were decorated with scenes from the Bible. The art of making stained glass is still practiced today, adding dramatic color to modern churches.

Renaissance painting

AFTER about 1300, great changes in art came about in Italy. Artists, sculptors, architects, and scholars began to rediscover the genius of the ancient Greek and Roman civilizations. This period of rediscovery became known as the Renaissance (French for "rebirth"). It lasted for over two centuries, gradually spreading throughout Europe. During the Renaissance, artists discovered new ways of copying the real world more accurately.

◨ OIL PAINTING

Oil painting was developed in northern Europe after about 1400. The oil allowed artists to blend their colors smoothly, and to show the delicate effect of light through gentle shading. As a result, figures became more three-dimensional, as in this Madonna and Child by Italian artist Giovanni Bellini (1430–1516).

◪ PERSPECTIVE

During the Renaissance, for the first time, artists became aware of the rules of "perspective," which allow three-dimensional space to be shown realistically in a flat painting. They realized that things appear smaller the farther away they are, and that the parallel lines of buildings point towards a "vanishing point"—as in this painting by Domenico di Bartolo (c.1400–44).

◩ RUBENS

Italy remained the great center for European art throughout the Renaissance. Artists from northern Europe went there to learn, including Flemish painter Pieter-Paul Rubens (1577–1640), famous for his lively works.

◪ CARAVAGGIO

Oil paint allowed artists to create the colors of very deep, dark shadows, as well as strong or subtle light effects—a technique known as chiaroscuro (meaning "light-dark"). The great master of chiaroscuro was the Italian Michelangelo Merisi da Caravaggio (1571–1610). His *Supper at Emmaus* depicts Christ's reappearance after the Crucifixion.

◪ BOTTICELLI

In medieval times, most art was paid for by the Church. But during the Renaissance, wealthy rulers became patrons of the arts. This meant that artists could paint new subjects that were not religious, such as portraits, battle scenes, and pictures from Greek and Roman mythology. A famous example is the *Birth of Venus* (the Roman goddess of love) by the Italian Sandro Botticelli (c.1444–1510).

◪ HOLBEIN

One of the greatest portrait painters of the Renaissance was the German artist Hans Holbein the Younger (c.1497–1543). He painted many of the most famous people of his times in minute detail, including King Henry VIII of England, shown here. Holbein lived in England after 1532.

THE GENIUS OF LEONARDO DA VINCI

The greatest Renaissance artists were not just painters and sculptors, but also gifted architects, engineers, poets, and musicians. One of the most famous is the Italian Leonardo da Vinci (1452–1519). Although celebrated as a painter, he only completed about 25 paintings. He spent much of his time making drawings of his inventions—such as this flying machine, multibarreled guns, a parachute, and even a tank.

The early 19th century

THE skills of painters continued to develop after the age of Rubens (1577–1640). Some artists perfected their technique for imitating the real world in the finest detail. Others, such the great Dutch painter Rembrandt van Rijn (1606–69), showed how artists could also convey mood, atmosphere, and personal feeling in their work. These two tendencies—technical clarity and artistic expression—remained the central themes in the changing styles of art during the early 19th century.

◪ PARIS SALON
By the 19th century, the focus of European art had switched from Italy to France. Each year, the public crowded into the exhibitions of the French Royal Academy of Painting and Sculpture, called the Salon, to see the latest works, as shown in this painting by François Biard (1798–1882).

◩ JACQUES-LOUIS DAVID
One of the leading French painters in about 1800 was Jacques-Louis David (1748–1825). He tried to re-create the glory of ancient Roman and Greek times with a grand style called Neoclassicism. This heroic mood is seen in his portrait of the French leader, *Napoleon Crossing the Alps* (1800).

◪ GUSTAVE COURBET
Until the 1850s, only a limited range of subjects was thought to be "noble" enough for fine art—history, Greek and Roman mythology, landscapes, and flattering portraits. The French painter Gustave Courbet (1819–77) reacted against this by painting ordinary, working people and the hardships of their daily lives, as seen in *The Corn-Sifters* (1865). He called this new approach "Realism."

ART AND BEAUTY

The English painter Edward Burne-Jones (1833–98) took a very different view of art to Courbet's Realism. He wrote: "I mean by a picture a beautiful romantic dream, of something that never was, never will be—in a light better than any that ever shone—in a land no one can define...."

☑ FORMAL TRAINING

In France, artists were trained to paint in schools called academies. The teachers were often very gifted artists, who could paint with technical brilliance. But the strict teaching rules of these schools tended to stifle personal flair, and artists who trained in them often produced technically correct, but dull work.

◁ THÉODORE GÉRICAULT

During the decades around 1800, a movement called Romanticism influenced both paintings and writing. It championed feelings—emotion, love, despair, the sublime. One of the most famous paintings of the time was *The Raft of the Medusa* (1819), by French artist Théodore Géricault (1791–1824), which depicts the ordeal of the survivors of a real-life shipwreck.

☐ PRE-RAPHAELITES

In 1848, a group of English artists began a movement called the Pre-Raphaelite Brotherhood, hoping to re-create the simplicity of early Italian art before the time of Raphael (1483–1520). They painted romantic pictures of great technical brilliance, often of scenes from the Bible, or from mythology or medieval history. *The Mirror of Venus* is by the English painter Edward Burne-Jones.

The late 19th century

DURING the 1870s, a new, energetic art movement developed in France. A group of painters, including Claude Monet (1840–1926), Pierre-Auguste Renoir (1841–1919), Camille Pissarro (1830–1903), and Alfred Sisley (1839–99), set out to paint the world around them. To capture a sense of immediacy, they painted outdoors and quickly, using rapid brushstrokes. Their movement was called "Impressionism." It changed forever the way that European artists approached painting.

◄ RENOIR

A painting such as *The Swing* (1876), by Renoir, shows how the Impressionists built up their pictures using dabs of color, rather than strong shapes and lines. They shared a desire to capture on canvas the visual effects of dappled sunlight, and used blue instead of black for shadows.

▲ SYMBOLISM

In contrast to the Impressionists, who painted the world they saw around them, many later artists wanted to paint the world of the imagination. Works by artists such as the French painter Paul Sérusier (1864–1927) evoked the mood of dreams, myths, and poetry.

◱ VAN GOGH

The Dutch painter Vincent van Gogh (1853–90) adopted the Impressionist style of painting. But he also conveyed a new sense of intense feeling in his work, seen in the vigorous dabs and swirls of paint in *Siesta* (1889–90). Because he took Impressionism one step further, Van Gogh is known as a "Post-Impressionist" (*post* meaning "after" in Latin).

◪ MONET

The Impressionists exhibited together for the last time in 1886, after which other styles of art took over. But Claude Monet lived on for another 40 years, always experimenting with the Impressionist style, and creating vibrant fields of color, as in his waterlily series of paintings.

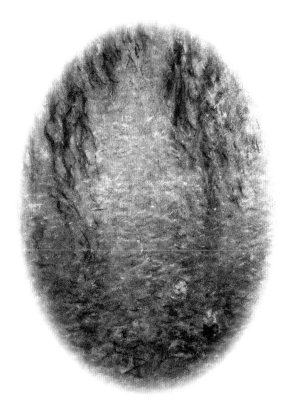

◪ POINTILLISM

The French artist Georges Seurat (1859–91) took the Impressionist technique to its logical conclusion. Instead of using dabs of paint, he created paintings made up entirely of tiny dots of color, as seen in his *Circus Parade* (1887–88). This style is known as Pointillism.

◪ BRUSHWORK

Impressionist artists broke away from the European tradition of realistic, detailed work, and felt free to apply paint in any way they chose. Vigorous brushstrokes, as in this harbor scene by the Spanish painter Joaquin Sorolla y Bastida (1863–1923), gave their work a vibrant sense of movement.

NOT APPRECIATED

Van Gogh's works, such as his sunflower paintings, are now worth millions. But in his lifetime they were not appreciated at all. Mentally disturbed, he committed suicide in 1890, having sold just one painting.

The 20th century

IN THE early 1900s, young artists began to explore new ways of painting. They stopped trying to imitate the real world, which had been the main aim of art since the Renaissance, and instead experimented with bright, unrealistic colors and shapes, rearranging the spaces that we see in the real world. The Cubists explored ways of showing how something might look if it was broken down into geometric shapes, such as cubes, and viewed from several different angles at once. Other artists made "abstract art" by arranging shapes and colors.

◪ PICASSO
The Spanish artist Pablo Picasso (1881–1973) was one of the leaders of the Cubist movement, which lasted from 1907 to about 1914. He is celebrated as perhaps the greatest artist of the 20th century.

◪ CUBISM
One of the three main Cubist painters was the Spaniard Juan Gris (1887–1927), whose *Landscape, Ceret* (1913) is shown here. Cubism challenged the traditional use of perspective, which allowed three-dimensional space to be shown on a flat surface. Instead, the subject of the painting was broken up into shapes, which were then rearranged.

◪ JACKSON POLLOCK
In the second half of the 20th century, the focus of modern art shifted from Europe to the United States. A leading figure was Jackson Pollock (1912–56). He created large, abstract pictures by splashing paint onto a canvas on the floor—a style known as Abstract Expressionism.

SURREALISM

During the 1920s, a group of artists set out to paint images of the unconscious mind, creating bizarre, dreamlike pictures, often in lifelike detail. One of these "surrealists" was the Belgian painter René Magritte (1898–1967), who also enjoyed playing with words. His picture of a pipe was labeled "This is not a pipe."

◨ DALI

The Spanish painter Salvador Dali (1904–89) is famous for his strange, dreamlike paintings with oddly extended bodies, melting watches, and half-open drawers set in desert landscapes, all painted in meticulous detail. He became the best known of the surrealists, partly because his real life was almost as bizarre as his paintings.

◧ EXPRESSIONISM

The style of painting known as Expressionism began in Germany and France in about 1905. Painters expressed emotions with strong colors, vigorous brushstrokes, and distorted images. *The Harvest* (1928) is by Constant Permeke (1885–1952), a leading Belgian Expressionist.

◨ COLLAGE

The word "collage" comes from the French *coller*—"to stick." In their efforts to break away from traditional ways of painting, the Cubists began to stick printed words, music, and bits of wallpaper into their works. The Surrealists, such as the German Max Ernst (1891–1976), took this a step further, and created whole pictures out of images cut from printed books and magazines.

Techniques of painting

THE changing styles of painting over the centuries have often reflected the kinds of materials that were available to artists. For instance, the Impressionists were able to paint landscapes in the open air because, after 1841, oil paint was sold in small, easily portable tubes. Each kind of paint—oil paint, watercolor, or modern water-based acrylic— behaves in a different way, and produces its own distinctive effects.

◨ FRESCO

To create murals that would last for decades or even centuries, medieval artists in Italy, such as Giotto, applied water-based paint to plaster that was still wet, or fresh. The technique was called fresco (from the Italian for fresh). Painters had to color small patches of plaster before it dried.

◨ OIL PAINT

With oil paint, the color, or "pigment," is mixed with an oil such as clove or linseed oil. The paint can be applied very thickly, so the brushstrokes still show. Vincent van Gogh used this technique, known as "impasto," in the painting shown here. Thick oil paint may take many weeks to dry fully.

◨ ARTISTS' MATERIALS

Artists using oil paints work on a canvas, which is stretched over a wooden frame and propped on an easel. Using an animal-hair brush, they mix the colors on their palette, perhaps adding turpentine to make it thinner.

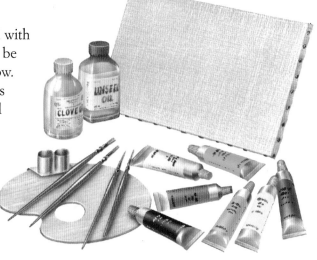

▣ WATERCOLOR

With watercolor, the pigment is mixed with water and then applied to paper. Watercolor paints are easy to carry around, and they dry quickly. But it is hard to correct mistakes. One of the greatest watercolorists was the English painter John Sell Cotman (1782–1842), who painted *The Ruins of Rievaulx Abbey* in 1803.

☑ COLOR WHEEL

The three primary colors are red, yellow, and blue. These can be mixed together to form orange, green, and purple. On a color wheel, one primary color will appear opposite the mixture of the two other primary colors (for example, red will appear opposite green, which is a mixture of yellow and blue). These opposites are called complementary colors.

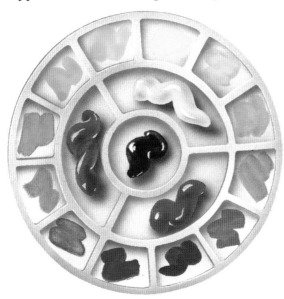

☑ MIXING COLORS

Modern paints are manufactured in many shades, based on mixtures of the primary colors, as well as black and white. They have special names, such as burnt umber, cadmium yellow, cobalt blue, and phthalo green. These can be mixed together to produce just about any color found in nature. As a rule, artists mix colors on their palette before applying them to the painting.

PIGMENTS

In the past, the color (or pigment) used in paints was based on naturally occurring substances, such as extracts of plants. Today, many pigments are made using synthetic chemical dyes, such as the phthalocyanine used to make phthalo green (shown here).

Printed art

Most paintings are made as individual pieces of work. This gives them extra value, but generally means few people see the work. The advantage of printing is that an image can be reproduced many times. People have known how to print since ancient times. By cutting an image into a flat surface—such as a block of wood or stone, or even a slice of potato—and then smearing it with ink, the image can be transferred to paper many times over. In Europe, printing has been used to mass-produce art since the 15th century.

WOODBLOCKS

The Japanese became very skilled at making woodblock prints. In the 19th century, Ando Hiroshige (1797–1858) produced a series of famous landscapes. Each color was applied separately, using as many as 20 blocks to make each print.

ANDY WARHOL

One of the most famous modern artists to use printing was the American Andy Warhol (1928–87). In his "Pop Art," he chose as his subjects mass-market images such as soup cans, and printed multiple copies of them using the silkscreen process.

ENGRAVING

This early 19th-century print was made in Austria using a method called engraving. To make an engraving, lines were cut into a metal plate with a sharp tool called a burin. Ink was then rubbed into the lines, so they could be printed onto paper. Colors were usually painted in later by hand.

Der Musik Unterricht

1. Plate is coated with varnish and smoothed

2. An image is scratched into the varnish

3. Plate is immersed in an acid bath

4. Varnish is removed

☑ LITHOGRAPHY

In the method of printing called lithography (after the Greek *lithos*, "stone"), originally the image was drawn onto stone with a wax crayon, then the stone was covered in water. When oily printer's ink was applied, it ran off the water, but stuck to the wax, so the image could be transferred to paper. Modern color printing uses metal sheets, but the same principles apply.

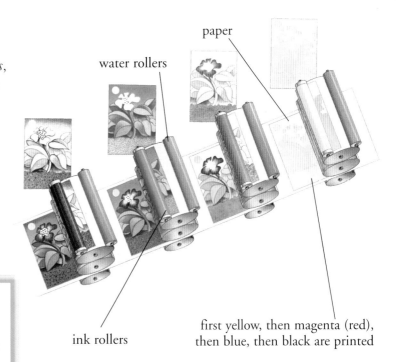

water rollers

paper

ink rollers

first yellow, then magenta (red), then blue, then black are printed

TOULOUSE-LAUTREC

Lithography was invented in 1798, and artists were quick to see its advantages. It allowed them to draw freely, in a way that was not possible with other printing methods. The French painter Henri de Toulouse-Lautrec (1841–1901) used lithography to produce his famous posters, such as this one advertising a new novel (1892).

☑ SILKSCREEN

In silkscreen printing, a stencil image is cut out of paper and stuck to a fine-mesh screen that has been stretched over a frame. The screen is laid over a blank sheet of paper, and ink is pushed across the screen using a rubber blade. This ensures that the image is transferred evenly to the paper.

☑ ETCHING

Etching is an old printing method in which acid is used to "etch," or bite into, metal. First, a copper plate is covered in a kind of acid-resistant varnish. The artist creates an image by scratching through the varnish to the metal. The plate is covered with acid, which cuts into the metal only where the artist has drawn. Then the plate is cleaned and rubbed with ink, so the lines can be printed onto paper.

5. Ink is pressed onto plate

6. Excess ink is wiped away

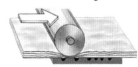

7. Paper is laid over plate and pressed with a roller

Stone sculpture

SCULPTURE may be an even older form of art than painting. Small limestone sculptures, such as the Venus of Willendorf, found in Austria, date back to 25,000 BC. Stone is hard to carve, but sculptures made from it have one great advantage—they last just about forever. Long after virtually all other remains of a civilization have rotted away, the stone sculptures survive. This is why stone sculpture has played such an important part in the history of art and civilization.

☑ GREEK SCULPTURE

The ancient Greeks were the greatest sculptors of the ancient world. They used sculpture to decorate their temples. This head of Medusa was found at the Temple of Apollo at Didyma, Turkey. The Greeks were also expert at turning stone—usually the fine stone called marble— into lifelike imitations of real people.

◪ EGYPTIAN GODS

The ancient Egyptians developed their own style of religious sculpture, which followed sacred rules. It was usually rather stiff and formal, like this pair of gods, Seth and Nephthys, sculpted during the time of Ramses II, who reigned about 1292–25 BC.

☑ ROMAN SCULPTURE

The Romans followed the Greek approach to sculpture, and many Greek sculptors went to work in Rome. The realistic, life-sized marble sculpture of *The Dying Gaul* is a Roman copy of a Greek bronze statue made about 220 BC.

◄ MODERN SCULPTURE

Not all ancient cultures tried to imitate real life in their art. This was the case with the sculpture of ancient Mexico. Modern sculptors likewise have taken a much freer and more imaginative approach to their work, not only in Mexico—where this work comes from—but all over the world. They shifted away from the idea of imposing a specific meaning on the stone, to one of working with the material, letting it guide them. Abstract sculpture did not become common until the 1950s.

◭ MICHELANGELO

Inspired by Roman sculpture that was found during the Renaissance, the Italian artist Michelangelo Buonarroti (1475–1564) became the greatest sculptor in stone since ancient times. He could turn blocks of marble into extraordinarily lifelike and tender works. His figure of *Moses* was created for the tomb of Pope Julius II (c.1513–45).

◄ CLAY SCULPTURE

Baked clay can last almost as long as stone, although it is more easily broken. This clay model of a potter comes from the Bahia culture of Ecuador, and is at least 1,500 years old. There is an important difference between clay sculpture and stone sculpture, however. Stone sculpture is created by chipping away from a block of stone, whereas clay sculpture is made by manipulating—or "modeling"— the clay while it is still soft.

VENUS DE MILO
One of the most famous pieces of ancient Greek sculpture, carved in about 150 BC, now stands in the Louvre in Paris. It was found on a beach on the Greek island of Milos in 1820. It is thought to represent the Greek ideal of female beauty.

Bronze sculpture

AN ANCIENT method of making long-lasting sculpture was to cast it in metal. First of all, the sculptor has to make the original model, usually out of a soft material that is easy to carve, such as clay, plaster, or wax. Then a mold is made, usually by wrapping the model in clay. Last, molten metal is poured into the mold, so it takes the shape of the original model. Methods like these have been used to cast sculpture in gold and copper, but the usual metal used for sculpture is bronze, which is a mixture of copper and tin.

◁ INCA GOLD

The Inca civilization, which flourished in the Andes Mountains of South America more than 500 years ago, made jewelry, tools, and delicate sculptures from gold, such as this small religious figure. To do this, they often used the "lost wax method." First, a model was made from beeswax. This was covered in clay, which made a mold. When the mold was heated, the wax melted and drained away. It was replaced with molten gold.

◣ PLASTER MODEL

One of the greatest sculptors of the late 19th century was Auguste Rodin (1840–1917) of France. He was famous for his lifelike statues, made in stone or bronze. His biggest project was *The Gates of Hell*, for a Paris museum. He never finished it, but after his death several bronze casts were made from his plaster model.

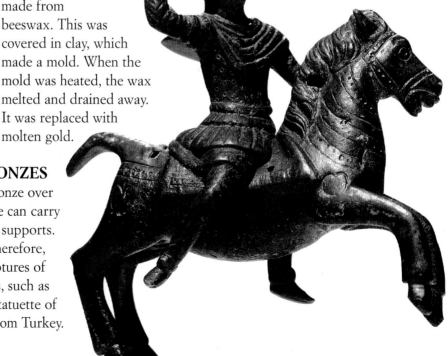

◻ EARLY BRONZES

One advantage of bronze over marble is that bronze can carry heavy weights on thin supports. Bronze was ideal, therefore, for making sculptures of horses and their riders, such as this first-century-BC statuette of a horseman from Turkey.

▶ BRONZE CASTING

In ancient times, bronze was used to make weapons and tools. First, rocks containing copper and tin ores were mined from underground. These were heated until the metals melted and could be separated from the rocks. Ingots of copper and tin were then heated together to make bronze. The molten bronze was poured into a mold. "Casting" the bronze into an object was a highly skilled job.

copper and tin ores are heated together

bronze sword

molten bronze is poured into mold

◀ SCULPTURE AND ARCHITECTURE

Modern engineering techniques have allowed artists to create sculpture on a huge scale. The *Atomium*, shown here, was built for the international fair held in Brussels in 1958. Its nine huge steel balls, rising to 396 feet (120 meters), represent a giant model of an atom.

▶ HENRY MOORE

Henry Moore (1898–1986) was Britain's leading 20th-century sculptor. His work was usually based on the human form, as in his bronze *King and Queen* (1952–53). But sometimes his figures were less easily recognized, and appear as rounded shapes pierced with holes.

GIACOMETTI

The Swiss sculptor Alberto Giacometti (1901–66) was famous for his bronze figures, which he began to produce in 1947. Their thin, fragile-looking bodies and long arms and legs show the rough surface of the clay models from which they were cast.

Photography

THE oldest surviving photograph was taken in 1827. Cameras and photographic techniques developed rapidly in the decades that followed. By the 1860s, it was possible to take very good portraits and landscape pictures in black and white, and some photographers were beginning to see photography as an art form. This was one reason why the Impressionists and later artists decided that they had to do more with painting than simply copy reality, which photography could do better.

◪ CARTE DE VISITE

Photography enabled people to have affordable pictures of themselves for the first time. During the 1860s, hundreds of photographic studios were set up around the world to take portrait photographs the size of a visiting card, or *carte de visite*. Millions of portraits were taken—a craze that was known as "cartomania."

hole collects image of the outside world and mirror projects it into the room

dark room

light table

projected image on light table

◪ CAMERA OBSCURA

The word "camera" comes from an old invention called a camera obscura (Latin for "dark room")—a room in which a "live" picture of the outside world is projected onto a dish through a small hole in the roof. The breakthrough of photography was the discovery of a way to capture this picture permanently, using light-sensitive chemicals.

◪ PHOTOGRAPHY AND ART

Photography came to influence many painters. The French artist Edgar Degas (1834–1917) tried to imitate the more spontaneous, unposed compositions often seen in photographs.

◤ HENRI CARTIER-BRESSON
The French photographer Henri Cartier-Bresson (b.1908) is celebrated for his numerous unusual compositions of 20th-century people and events. Many of his pictures contain a number of points of interest—rather like this photo of him in New York, holding his famous Leica camera.

◤ DAGUERREOTYPE
The pioneers of early photography experimented with various methods. The daguerreotype was invented by Frenchman Louis Daguerre (1789–1851) in 1839. It produced excellent photographs on silver-coated copper sheets, but as there were no negatives, it was hard to make copies.

◄ FASHION PHOTOGRAPHY
Photography has been used in magazines and for advertising since the 1880s. During the 20th century, many of the most famous photographers, such as the American Richard Avedon (b.1923), worked for fashion magazines like *Vogue*. In this 1960s edition, held by dress designer Mary Quant, the cover girl is the famous model Twiggy.

WAR PHOTOGRAPHY
Photographs have helped to show the grim, unglamorous side of war since 1855, when British photographer Roger Fenton took pictures of the Crimean War. Famous war photographers include the American Robert Capa (1913–54), who captured dramatic images of the Spanish Civil War and World War II.

Applied art

THE kind of paintings and sculpture found in museums and galleries is often referred to as "fine art." But a great deal of artistic creativity is also devoted to making ordinary or practical objects more beautiful—through what is known as "applied art." Fountains, for example, have a practical function, and yet they may spout from magnificent and elaborate works of sculpture. By and large, artists either make fine art or applied art, but some do both.

◿ SALT CELLAR

Benvenuto Cellini (1500–71) was a brilliant goldsmith and sculptor, and also one of the most wild and colorful characters of the Italian Renaissance. He created this magnificent piece for the king of France—as something to hold the salt on the dining table!

◿ PORCELAIN FIGURE

Great skills in both sculpture and painting have been applied to pottery figurines, created to decorate the living rooms of collectors. This Kakiemon porcelain figure of a man was made in Japan during the Edo period (1615–1867).

◿ TAPESTRY

Woolen wall hangings, or tapestries, had a practical purpose—they helped to keep rooms warm in the days before central heating. From medieval times on, expensive European tapestries were designed to look like paintings, often by great artists such as Rubens, and were woven by skilled craftworkers. These huge 17th-century tapestries are in the Château of Fontainebleau in France.

◢ JEWELRY

Careful design and fine craftsmanship have been applied to jewelry since ancient times. Beauty is, after all, a key feature of jewelry. In about 1900, the fashionable style called Art Nouveau brought a fresh, swirling elegance to jewelry design, as seen in this belt buckle and hair comb.

◰ WALLPAPER

During the 19th century, improved manufacturing techniques made it possible to produce lower-cost wallpaper. Good wallpaper patterns have a sense of balance and graceful elegance, like those produced by the English designer William Morris (1834–96), who based his designs on shapes drawn from nature. His work influenced many other designers, such as C.F.A. Voysey (1857–1941), who designed this wallpaper in 1909.

MURALS

Long before wallpaper was invented, walls were decorated with murals. The Etruscans, who lived in Italy before the Roman period, painted their tombs with delightful scenes of their lives and pleasures. Their homes may have been similarly decorated, but only the tombs have survived.

◳ ISLAMIC TILEWORK

Muslim designers became very skilled at making patterns, particularly with glazed tiles. Generally, these were used on the inside walls and floors of buildings, but in Isfahan, in Iran, tiles also cover the domes of the mosques. This is the Royal Mosque of Abbas I, built from about 1590 to 1629. The bright blue color of some of the tiles is also typical of the pottery of the region.

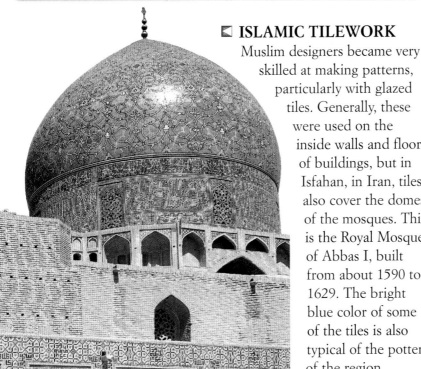

Commercial art

MOST artists find it hard to earn a living by selling paintings or sculpture. Many gifted painters instead use their skills to create the illustrations needed in the world of business—for example, advertising, packaging, CD covers, illustrated storybooks, magazine articles, and instruction manuals. Illustrators are generally not able to choose what they draw or paint, but instead must follow instructions from the person who is buying their "artwork." They are briefed to create images for a specific task.

◥ COMIC STRIPS

Stories told in pictures have existed since ancient times. The hilarious storybook *Struwelpeter* (from which this illustration is taken) was written by the German writer Heinrich Hoffmann in 1845. It was a forerunner of the first comics for children, which appeared in the 1890s.

◥ FAIRY TALES

Illustrations for children's books became more elaborate as the techniques of color printing improved. The gifted British illustrator, painter, and caricaturist Richard Doyle (1824–83) produced this picture for a book called *Adventures in Fairyland*.

◢ ADVERTISING

Art has played a role in advertising since the early days of printing in the 1500s. Businesses soon realized that mass-produced posters could attract more public attention if they included a striking picture, as on this 1930s advertisement for tea.

BUY INDIAN TEA

EMB

◩ POSTERS

Some of the most famous posters in the history of advertising were produced in Paris in the late 19th century, at the time when Toulouse-Lautrec was making his lithographs. An 1898 poster for the celebrated nightspot the Folies Bergère, by Paul Berthon (1848–1909), is typical of the era.

Münchner illustrierte Wochenschrift für Kunst und Leben. — G. Hirth's Verlag in München & Leipzig.

◩ MAGAZINES

Hundreds of illustrated magazines were launched in the 19th century, benefiting from cheaper printing and a wide distribution by trains. This edition of the illustrated weekly *Jugend* ("Youth") was published in Germany in 1897.

◪ LOGO

Artistic design is applied to company "logos," such as the VW badge that appears on Volkswagen cars. The best logos are simple, but instantly recognizable—and are much harder to design than most people imagine.

COMPUTER ART

The computer is a powerful new tool for artists. Because of their huge memories, computers can generate and alter a vast range of images, at great speed.

The art world

A GREAT many people are involved in the world of art, including those who buy and sell paintings and sculpture, those who work in galleries, and the art directors who commission illustrations for magazines and other publications. But the most important people of all are the artists who create the paintings, sculpture, and other works of art. In the technical and commercial age of the 21st century, the world needs their creative talent as much as it ever has.

◪ NORMAN ROCKWELL
The work of commercial artists is generally not valued as highly as the work of the great masters. One exception was the American painter Norman Rockwell (1894–1978). He was famous for his images of American life, painted for the cover of *The Saturday Evening Post*.

◪ THE ARTIST'S STUDIO
Most artists paint in a special room called a studio. In the past, the most famous artists had big studios, like that of Rubens, shown here. They employed numerous assistants to help them.

◪ THE LOUVRE
The Louvre in Paris contains one of the world's greatest collections of European art. Once a royal palace, it was extended in the 17th century to house the growing royal collection, which the public was allowed to visit after 1681. In 1989, it was given a new, ultramodern entrance under a glass pyramid.

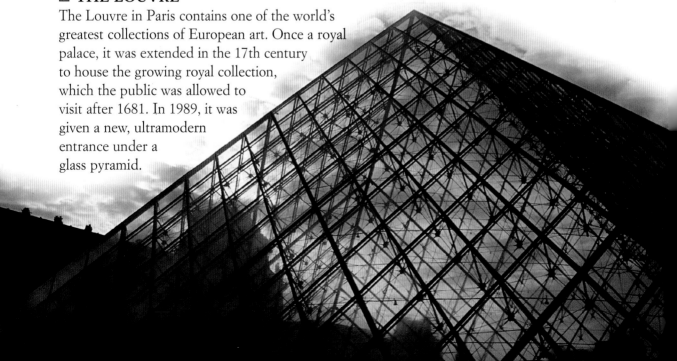

AUCTIONS

Many works of art by the old masters are owned by private collectors. If they want to sell one, they usually go to a leading auction house, where, on an advertised date, the work is sold to the highest bidder.

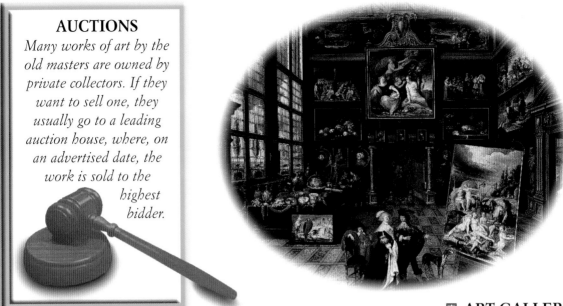

ART GALLERIES

Originally, galleries were places where private collectors of art kept their paintings and sculpture. Art dealers also had galleries, where collectors could view works of art that were for sale. The pictures often covered the walls, as in this 17th-century painting. The first public galleries were opened in the 1600s.

ROYAL COLLECTIONS

Fine art is considered to be a symbol of wealth, culture, and good taste. The Queen of England has inherited a large and very valuable collection, including works by Leonardo da Vinci, Michelangelo, Holbein, Rubens, and many others. They can be seen at Buckingham Palace (shown here) and Windsor Castle.

STREET ART

Some artists do not make art that can be collected. Street artists draw in chalk on the sidewalk, and collect small gifts of money from admiring passers-by. At the end of the day, the picture is erased, or washed away by the rain.

Glossary

ABSTRACT ART
Paintings that have no obvious similarity to real objects, made by arranging shapes and colors in a purely imaginary way that may be hard to understand.

ARCHAEOLOGISTS
Experts who find out how people lived in the past, by digging up and studying the places where they lived, and the remains they left behind.

ART NOUVEAU
French phrase meaning "new art," an elegant design style of natural flowing, or swirling lines, fashionable at the beginning of the 20th century.

CAMERA OBSCURA
A windowless room or box with a small hole in one wall, through which light passes from outside, to produce on the wall opposite inside, an upside-down (inverted) image of the scene outside.

CARICATURIST
An artist, writer, or performer who produces grotesque, often humorous pictures or portraits of people which greatly exaggerate their features and characteristics.

CHIAROSCURO
"Bright-dark," a painting or drawing technique that creates strong light-and-shadow effects using subtle colors.

COMMISSION
To order a picture or other piece of work to be created, often specially for and to the instructions of the person making the order.

CUBISM
A 20th-century painting technique where the image is broken down into geometric shapes like circles, squares, and cubes, which are then rearranged in the picture.

DISCIPLE
A follower or pupil of a leader or teacher, or a philosophy or faith; often used for the first followers of Jesus Christ, especially the twelve Apostles.

ENGRAVING
A printing technique where a pattern or image is cut, or engraved, into a metal or wooden plate, ink is then rubbed on, and the plate is pressed onto paper to make an impression.

ETCHING
A printing technique where a pattern or image is cut into an acid-proof coating on a metal plate, and acid is applied, which etches, or erodes, the image into the metal. Then the coating is removed and the plate used to make prints.

EXPRESSIONISM
A style of drama, music, or painting where the artist or performer tries to illustrate or express emotions and feelings, rather than real images of the actual world.

FRESCO
From the Italian word for "fresh," a painting done on the plaster or render (coating) of a wall or ceiling using water-based paints, which are applied while the plaster is still wet.

ICONS
Sacred images from Christianity, such as Christ, Mary, one of the saints, or a scene from the Bible—sculpted or painted onto wooden panels and used as a centerpiece for prayer and worship.

ILLUMINATIONS
Paintings of characters, especially those made by medieval monks, to illustrate handwritten books, often to emphasize the first letter on a page.

IMPASTO
A technique of applying oil or acrylic paint so thickly, with a brush or a palette knife, that the texture and thickness of the strokes remain in the paint.

IMPRESSIONISM
A technique developed by French artists in the 19th century, who painted very quickly outside, using tiny dabs of paint to give an idea of the subject, rather than a detailed and realistic image.

LITHOGRAPHY
A printing technique where an image is drawn in wax or oil onto a slab of stone or metal, and after treatment with chemicals, such as acid and water, ink sticks only to the waxed or oiled areas, and can then be transferred to paper.

LOGO
An emblem, design, or symbol used by an organization, which appears on things concerned with that organization, such as buildings, vehicles, and clothing.

MEDIEVAL
Usually referring to the Middle or Dark Ages, a 1000-year period in history, which generally began at the end of the Roman era, around AD 400, and ended with the Renaissance, around AD 1400.

MONKS
Men who have chosen to devote their lives to worship and prayer, and who live together in a religious community and follow strict rules, such as poverty and obedience.

MOSAICS
Decorative patterns or pictures made by arranging pieces of colored glass, tiles, or stones, often bedding them into cement or mortar to be firmly held.

MOSQUE
A building where Muslims (followers of Islam) meet to worship, pray, and listen to readings from the Holy Book, the *Qu'ran*.

MURAL
A painting made to decorate a wall, which may be applied directly to the surface, such as the rock of a cave, or the plaster of a wall, or to canvas, which is then stuck onto the wall.

MYTHOLOGY
Collections of traditional stories used to describe and explain the history of a people or group, often involving gods, goddesses, heroes, and heroines.

NEOCLASSICISM
A grand 19th-century style of painting that tried to re-create the formal artistic glory or classical tradition of ancient Greece and Rome.

ORES
Naturally occurring substances that can be dug or mined from the ground, and from which metals or other valuable minerals can be extracted.

PATRON
A rich person or benefactor who pays, gives gifts to, or otherwise assists a poorer but talented person, such as a musician, artist, composer, or actor.

PERSPECTIVE
The technique of illustrating the three-dimensional space of the real world on a two-dimensional flat surface, such as paper, for example, by showing things which are farther away as smaller, and making horizontal lines of walls, buildings, and fences lead away toward a single point on the horizon.

PIGMENT
A chemical that gives color to whatever contains it, for example, paints are made of finely ground crystalline pigments mixed with a base such as an oil.

PIONEER
Someone who does things that no one has done before, such as exploring unknown lands, or developing new musical styles or playing techniques.

PORCELAIN
A type of pottery invented in China more than 2,000 years ago, made from fine, white clay and ground glass, to produce delicate, thin-walled, translucent (almost see-through) items.

PREHISTORIC
The time from when the Earth began, or from a certain creation time, to when written records began, usually regarded as about 12,000–10,000 years ago.

PRIMARY COLORS
Red, yellow, and blue pigments, from which all other colors can be made by mixing them—but which cannot be made by mixing other colors.

REALISM
The 19th-century paintings of the real world, especially those of ordinary working people and their lives and hardships, which were subjects that previously had not been considered worthy of art.

RENAISSANCE
"Rebirth," the period in history after the medieval time of the "Dark Ages," when European artists and scholars began to rediscover and extend the classical knowledge of ancient Greeks and Romans; it generally dates from about AD 1400.

ROMANTICISM
Early 19th-century paintings and literature that illustrate powerful feelings and emotions, often suggesting a sentimental, "ideal," but unrealistic view, of reality.

SAINT
A person who was so good during life, that after death he or she still exists and becomes very holy, able to give guidance and answer people's prayers.

SURREALISM
A 20th-century painting style with strange, unreal, often dreamlike images, which may be inspired by deep thoughts or the unconscious mind.

SYMBOLISM
An artistic style of the late 19th century where painters used symbols, or representations, to suggest ideas that are inspired by the imagination rather than by the real world.

TAPESTRY
A thick piece of fabric on which a picture or pattern is created, either during the original weaving process, or by embroidery stitches added afterward.

TEMPLE
A building that is used for prayer and worship of a god, goddess, or similar revered person, or regarded as the place of residence of that person, or which has some other similar religious importance.

TRADITION
The passing on of the culture of a group of people from old to young, including their customs, stories, history, and beliefs.

TURPENTINE
An oily solvent made by distilling, or purifying, the resin from pine trees, that is often mixed with oil paints to make them thinner in consistency.

Index

ACKNOWLEDGMENTS

Art Archive: Page 9 (t/l) Dagli Orti, (b) Dagli Orti, 10 (b/r) Lucien Bitlon Collection Paris/Dagli Orti, 11 (t/l) Scrovegni Chapel Padua/Dagli Orti, (c/r) Art Archive, 12 (t/r) Santa Maria dlla Scala Hospital Siena/Dagli Orti, (c/l) Museo Correr Venice/Dagli Orti, (b) Museo del Prado Madrid/Art Archive, 13 (t/l) Galleria degli Uffizi Florence/Dagli Orti, (c/r) Galleria Brera Milan/Album/Joseph Martin, (b) Windsor Castle/Art Archive, 14 (t/r) Musée du Louvre Paris/Jaqueline Hyde, (c/l) Malmaison Musée du Chateau/Dagli Orti, (b/r) Musée de Beaux Arts Nantes/Dagli Orti, 15 (c/l) Musée du Louvre Paris/Dagli Orti, (b/r) Gulbenkian Foundation Lisbon/Dagli Orti, 16 (t/r) Musée d'Orsay Paris/Dagli Orti, (c/l) Musée du Louvre Paris/Dagli Orti, (b/r) Musée d'Orsay Paris/Dagli Orti, 17 (t/r) Metropolitan Museum of Art New York/Album/Joseph Martin, (c/l) Jean Walter & Paul Guillaume Coll/Dagli Orti, (b/r) Musée Sorolla Madrid/Album/Joseph Martin, 18 (b/r) Moderna Museet Stockholm/Dagli Orti, 19 (c/l) Konstant Parmeke Mus Jabbeke/Dagli Orti, 20 (t/r) Torre Aquila Trento/Dagli Orti, (c/l) Musée d'Orsay Paris/Dagli Orti, 21 (t/r) Victoria and Albert Museum London/Sally Chappell, 22 (c/l) Victoria and Albert Museum London/Sally Chappell, (b/r) Museum der Stadt Wien/Dagli Orti, 23 (b/l) Eileen Tweedy, 24 (t/l) Musée du Louvre Paris/Dagli Orti, (b) Museo Capitolino Rome/Dagli Orti, 25 (t/l) Dagli Orti, 26 (t/r) Musée d'Orsay Paris/Dagli Orti, (c/l) Museo del Oro Lima/Dagli Orti, (b/r) Middelheim Sculpture Garden Holland/Nicolas Sapieha, 27 (c/l) Dagli Orti, (b/r) Art Archive, 28 (b/r) Sao Paulo Art Museum Brazil/Dagli Orti, 29 (t/l) Victoria and Albert Museum London/Sally Chappell, 30 (t/r) Art Archive, (b) Dagli Orti, 31 (t/l) Private Collection/Dagli Orti, (c/l) Dagli Orti, (r) Victoria and Albert Museum London/Sally Chappell, 32 (t/r) Eileen Tweedy, (l) Eileen Tweedy, (b) Lords Gallery/Dagli Orti, 33 (t/r) Victoria and Albert Museum London/Eileen Tweedy, (c/l) Musée de l'Affiche Paris/Dagli Orti, 34 (c/l) Galleria della Uffizi Florence/Dagli Orti, 35 (t/r) Musée du Louvre Paris/Dagli Orti **Corbis:** Page 28 (t/r) Hulton-Deutsch Collection, 29 (c/r) Genevieve Naylor, (b/l) Bettmann, 35 (b/r) Robert Holmes

All other photographs are from:
MKP Archives; Corel Corporation; Photodisk

Other titles in this series:
**Design • History of Culture • Literature • Music
Myths and Legends • Performing Arts • Religion**